CONTENTS

COOKERY NOTES

- Both metric and imperial measures are given for the recipes. Follow either metric or imperial throughout as they are not interchangeable.
- All spoon measures are level unless otherwise stated. Sets of measuring spoons are available in metric and imperial for accurate measurement of small quantities.
- Ovens should be preheated to the specified temperature. Grills should also be preheated. The cooking times given in the recipes assume that this has been done.
- Where a stage is specified in brackets under freezing, the dish should be frozen at the end of that stage.
- Size 2 eggs should be used except where otherwise specified. Free-range eggs are recommended.
- Use freshly ground black pepper and sea salt unless otherwise specified.
- Use fresh rather than dried herbs unless dried herbs are suggested in the recipe.
- Stocks should be freshly made if possible. Alternatively buy ready-made stocks or use good quality stock cubes.

INTRODUCTION

Think of Italian food and you are immediately transported to the warm, sunny, scented air of the Mediterranean or a Sicilian orange grove, or the earthy sweetness of a wooded, vine and olive-covered Tuscan hill. In essence, to places visited on holiday with memories of carefree eating and drinking. The cooking is warm-hearted, simple and generous, the ingredients fresh and flavoursome and kissed by the sun.

In the main part the Italian kitchen doesn't suffer from produce that has been picked unripe from the other side of the world and transported in refrigerated containers to reach us with little of its true flavour. Most produce is homegrown, especially that which is sold in the markets, and is reliant on the seasons. As one season finishes, something else takes its place and so ingredients are that much more special – each season bringing its long awaited bounty.

There are seasons for fruit, vegetables, herbs, nuts, cheeses, types of bread and cakes, mushrooms, grapes, olives and wine. To some extent we have lost this way of life in Britain, but a visit to an Italian market will open your eyes. In summer the markets spill with tempting greenery. You will find all kinds of salad leaves, both wild and cultivated, including arugula (rocket), radicchio and chicory. Popular vegetables are beans, squash and pumpkin, aubergine, fennel, courgettes and their flowers for stuffing, potatoes and sweet peppers. All manner of fruits are available too, from large ripe, juicy melons and peaches to delicious sweet cherries and plump flavourful grapes.

It is impossible to cover the diversity of Italian food in a book like this, but I have tried to encompass the essence of Italian cooking in my recipes. Most are based on traditional dishes, but adapted to suit the tastes of today.

Italian cooking can be very simple, using the minimum of ingredients – as in Tuscan Bean Soup with Toasted Garlic and Olive Oil, for example. Other dishes, such as Seafood and Saffron Risotto, are more complex, but still employ the best native ingredients.

Italy has an extensive coastline, so it's hardly surprising that a wide variety of seafood is eaten. Squid, cuttlefish, sardines, anchovies, tuna, swordfish, red mullet, clams, mussels and prawns are popular.

Grilling is a favourite cooking method. Squid emerges tender and juicy in Char-Grilled Squid with Chillies and Aubergines. Polenta is grilled to give it a smoky flavour and is served with roasted game or meats, as in Pigeon on Crisp Polenta.

Game is popular throughout Italy, including rabbit, hare, wild boar and partridge, to name but a few. More meat is eaten in the north of the country where the climate and terrain favour rich cattle pastures. Rich Tuscan meat dishes, like Beef Braised in Barolo, and Italian Sausage Ragu with Soft Polenta, are great winter dishes.

As far as bread is concerned each area has its own specialities, from the saltless Tuscan bread to the ciabatta or slipper bread made with olive oil. Focaccia, which is eaten all over Italy, is really like a pizza bread and I have included a recipe with variations here. I've also given two pizza recipes – one without tomato and one with lots of topping. The latter isn't typically Italian as they are frugal with toppings! The staple filler foods of Italy – gnocchi, risotto and pasta – are all covered in this book. Vegetables are included too. These are always cooked very simply in Italy – with the minimum of extra ingredients – to bring out their true flavours, not to mask them.

No Italian book would be complete without a selection of desserts and baking recipes. Try the ridiculously rich Rice Ice Cream, silky smooth Panna Cotta with Strawberry Sauce or the lighter classic sorbets. Finish with homemade Biscotti – easy to make and a welcome gift!

I have tried to give a real taste of Italy in this book, introducing some new and exciting flavours and ideas to your cookery repertoire. I hope you enjoy them. Buon Appetito!

SPECIAL INGREDIENTS

ANCHOVIES

Whether salted or in oil, these are essential to give a piquant savouriness to some Italian dishes. Salted anchovies are preserved whole (without heads); they need to be rinsed and the backbone removed before using.

BALSAMIC VINEGAR

A rich sweet vinegar made from fermented Trebbiano grapes, aged in oak casks for at least 4 years, and in some cases, much longer. There is no real substitute, but sherry vinegar would do. Balsamic vinegar is especially good with strawberries.

CHEESE

Fresh mozzarella is a favourite for salads and pizzas – it melts to a delicious stringiness when heated; the best is made from water buffalo milk. *Parmigiano* or Parmesan is a hard *grana* cheese. It is salty and crumbly, and a pale straw colour. *Parmigiano Reggiano* is the best, but *Grana Padano* is good in cooking. Mascarpone is a fresh thick cheese made from cream, and used in desserts. Ricotta is a cheese made from whey and should be snowy white and sweet – it is also sold in a harder salted version. Ricotta is used in baking; it is also good in salads.

FLOUR

Italian breads such as Focaccia are made with ordinary plain flour; strong flour would give the wrong texture.

Pasta is traditionally made with Italian "00" flour (*Farina Tipo 00*) – the finest whitest grade of Italian *grano tenero* or soft grain flour. It is sometimes mixed with *semolino di grano duro* or semolina flour. This is made from the heart of the wheat, has a high gluten content and is the flour used for making commercial dried pasta. It gives pasta a firmer texture. It is good for 'flouring' fresh pasta as it is coarse-textured and aerates the dough prior to cooking.

Polenta flour, used for making soft polenta and firmer sliced grilled polenta, is coarsely ground maize. It takes a good 40 minutes to cook, but 'quick cook' polenta is available and takes only 5-10 minutes.

OLIVES, OIL, OLIVE PASTE

Olives are a much prized crop, picked late in the year when green, or left to ripen on the tree until black or purple. Olive oil is synonymous with Italian cuisine, and the choice is limitless. Choose a cold-pressed fruity extra virgin olive oil for dressing salads, and a lighter less expensive oil for cooking and baking. A dark green olive oil does not necessarily guarantee quality – taste it and see.

Olive pastes are rich and salty. They can be used as toppings or to flavour breads or pasta, or even whisked into salad dressings.

PROSCIUTTO, PANCETTA ETC

Prosciutto is the generic term for ham. *Prosciutto crudo* is raw cured ham, and Parma ham is a particularly high quality *prosciutto crudo*. Pancetta is unsmoked Italian bacon – smoked bacon should not be substituted.

RICE

Arborio rice for risotto is the most widely available exported Italian rice. It is a short-grain rice with good absorption and is essential for making creamy risottos.

SAUSAGES

These are freshly prepared at Italian delicatessens. They are made from coarsely ground pork, highly seasoned with salt and pepper. Chilli, basil and pine nuts are popular flavourings.

TOMATOES, SUN-DRIED, ETC

Fresh Italian plum tomatoes should be slightly soft, bright red and sweet. Canned and bottled tomatoes are essential in the winter when flavourful fresh ones are not available. Sun-dried tomatoes are used sparingly in Italian cooking and are not widely used. Tomato purée adds richness, and Sicilian *strattu*, a clay-like sun-dried concentrate of tomatoes, is a real find – a little goes a long way.

WILD MUSHROOMS, DRIED AND FRESH

The most famous and prized mushroom is the *porcini* or *cep*. It is gathered in the wild and much coveted. Both fresh and dried versions are expensive, but a few dried mushrooms, after soaking, add great flavour to risottos and sauces.

PASTA-MAKING

Freshly cooked homemade pasta is far superior to the commercially produced alternatives. For optimum results use type "00" flour (see page 6), and a pasta machine for rolling out and cutting. The following quantities are only a guideline: depending on the humidity, type of flour etc, you may need to add a little more flour. The dough must not be too soft – it should be quite hard to knead. Too much extra flour will make the pasta tough and taste floury!

200 g (7 oz) plain white flour
pinch of salt
2 (size 2) eggs
15 ml (1 tbsp) olive oil

1. Sift the flour and salt onto a clean work surface and make a well in the centre with your fist.

2. Beat the eggs and oil together and pour into the well.

3. Gradually mix the liquid ingredients into the flour, using the fingers of one hand.

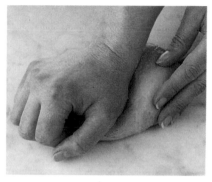

4. Knead the pasta until smooth. Wrap in cling film and allow to rest for at least 30 minutes before attempting to roll out; the pasta will be much more elastic after resting.

USING A FOOD PROCESSOR
Sift the flour and salt into the bowl. Pour in the beaten eggs and oil, together with any flavourings and process until the dough begins to come together. Turn out and knead until smooth. Wrap in cling film and rest for at least 30 minutes.

ROLLING OUT USING A PASTA MACHINE

1. Feed the rested dough through the widest setting several times.

2. Pass the pasta through the machine, narrowing the setting by one notch each time, until the required thickness is reached.

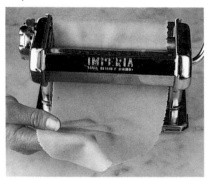

3. Generally the second from last setting is best for tagliatelle; the finest setting is used for ravioli or other pasta that is to be filled.

4. Once the required thickness is reached, hang the pasta over a piece of dowelling or a clean broom handle to dry a little; this will make cutting easier as the pasta won't be as sticky. If you are making stuffed pasta, drying isn't necessary because it needs to be slightly sticky to adhere properly.

5. Fit the appropriate cutters to the machine. Pass the pasta through, then transfer to a tray covered with a lightly floured clean tea-towel. Toss the pasta lightly in the flour and use as soon as possible. Alternatively, drape the pasta over the dowelling or broom handle again until ready to cook.

ROLLING OUT BY HAND

1. On a clean (not floured) surface, roll out one third of the dough to a 5 mm (¼ inch) thickness.

2. Lift the dough from the surface and rotate 45°. The dough should 'cling' (not stick) to the surface; this helps in the stretching process.

3. Continue rolling, lifting and rotating until the dough is very thin. Repeat with remaining dough.

TO COOK PASTA

As a guide, you will need 4 litres (7 pints) of water and 45 ml (3 tbsp) salt to every 350-450 g (12 oz-1 lb) fresh or dried pasta. A tablespoon of olive oil will help to stop the water boiling over and prevent the pasta sticking but, if you have enough water in the pan and you stir the pasta as it goes in, it will not stick.

1. Add the pasta to a large pan of boiling salted water and stir once to prevent sticking. Do not cover, or the water will boil over.

2. Quickly bring the pasta back to a rolling boil, stir once and boil until *al dente*, literally 'to the tooth'. The pasta should be just firm to the bite; it should not have a hard centre, nor should it be very floppy. Calculate the cooking time from the moment the pasta starts to boil again.

As a guide, fresh unfilled pasta, such as spaghetti and tagliatelle, usually takes 2-3 minutes to cook. But note that *very* thin pasta can be ready almost as soon as the water returns to the boil. Ordinary dried pasta generally cooks in 8-12 minutes, but it is important to keep checking as this is only a guide.

For fresh filled pasta, such as ravioli and tortelloni, allow 5-10 minutes; for dried, allow 15-20 minutes.

3. Quickly drain the pasta well using a large colander or sieve. Hold back 30-45 ml (2-3 tbsp) of the cooking water – this will help the sauce to cling to the pasta. Dress the pasta immediately with the sauce, oil or butter. Serve hot pasta straight away. It is up to you whether you toss the sauce before serving or serve it piled on top of the pasta. Either way, the pasta should be tossed with the sauce before eating!

VARIATIONS

SPINACH PASTA: Cook 140 g (5 oz) frozen leaf spinach and squeeze to remove as much moisture as possible. Proceed as for the basic pasta dough, blending the spinach with the 2 eggs, oil and a pinch of salt in a food processor or blender, before adding to the flour. You may need to use a little more flour to make a firm dough. Continue as for the basic recipe.

TOMATO PASTA: Add 30 ml (2 tbsp) tomato purée or sun-dried tomato paste to the flour with the eggs. Use size 3 eggs.

BEETROOT PASTA: Add 30 ml (2 tbsp) grated cooked beetroot to the flour with the eggs. Use size 3 eggs.

SAFFRON PASTA: Add a sachet of powdered saffron to 30 ml (2 tbsp) hot water and leave to soak for 15 minutes. Use size 3 eggs and whisk the saffron liquid into them.

HERB PASTA: Add 45 ml (3 tbsp) chopped fresh herbs to the flour.

BLACK INK PASTA: Add 1 sachet of squid ink to the eggs before adding to the flour. Use size 3 eggs.

TUSCAN BEAN SOUP WITH TOASTED GARLIC AND OLIVE OIL

Asubstantial white bean soup from Tuscany. Sliced garlic is fried in olive oil until golden, then poured over the soup at the last moment. It is often served as a main course ladled over toasted country bread. If the soup is thicker than you like, thin it down with a little extra water or stock.

SERVES 6

225 g (8 oz) dried white
  haricot or cannellini
  beans, soaked overnight in
  cold water
4 garlic cloves, peeled
150 ml (¼ pint) olive oil
salt and pepper
15-30 ml (1-2 tbsp)
chopped fresh parsley
  (optional)

PREPARATION TIME
20 minutes, plus overnight
soaking
COOKING TIME
About 1 hour 10 minutes
FREEZING
Suitable

330 CALS PER SERVING

1. Preheat the oven to 170°C (325°F) Mark 3. Drain the beans and place in a flameproof casserole. Cover with cold water to a depth of 5 cm (2 inches) above the beans. Bring to the boil, cover tightly and bake in the oven for about 1 hour or until tender (see note). Keep them in their cooking liquid.

2. Meanwhile, finely chop half the garlic and thinly slice the remainder.

3. Transfer half of the beans and liquid to a food processor or blender and process until smooth. Add this purée to the beans in the casserole and stir well.

4. Heat half the olive oil in a frying pan, add the chopped garlic and fry gently until soft and golden. Stir into the soup and reheat until boiling. Simmer gently for 10 minutes. Taste and season well with salt and pepper. Pour into a warmed tureen or individual soup bowls.

5. Heat the remaining olive oil in the frying pan and fry the sliced garlic until golden. Spoon over the soup and serve at once, sprinkled with chopped parsley if preferred.

NOTE: The cooking time depends on the freshness of the beans. Older beans will take longer to cook. Begin testing them after 45 minutes.

VARIATIONS

● Stir 4 skinned, seeded and chopped tomatoes into the soup as it is reheated.
● Stir 30 ml (2 tbsp) chopped fresh sage or rosemary into the soup with the puréed beans.

TECHNIQUE

Purée half of the beans and cooking liquid in a food processor or blender.

FRITTO MISTO

Juicy morsels of seafood – coated in the lightest, crispest batter – are served piping hot with a squeeze of lemon and a glass of chilled white wine. Italian immigrants, to Scotland in particular, found a new career in making and selling fish and chips – a legacy of their *fritto misto* in far away Italy.

SERVES 6

BATTER

200ml (7 fl oz) water

75 g (3 oz) plain white flour

salt

FRITTO MISTO

1 litre (1¾ pints) fresh
   mussels in shells, cleaned
   (see page 20)

175 g (6 oz) squid, cleaned
   (see page 38)

175 g (6 oz) small sole or
   red mullet fillets, skinned

175 g (6 oz) medium raw
   prawns

175 g (6 oz) whitebait

oil for deep-frying

TO SERVE

lemon wedges

PREPARATION TIME
20 minutes
COOKING TIME
15 minutes
FREEZING
Not suitable

325 CALS PER SERVING

1. To make the batter, pour the water into a shallow bowl. Sift the flour with a good pinch of salt over the surface of the water. Whisk well until smooth; the batter should have the consistency of double cream. Set aside. Preheat the oven to a low setting.

2. Put the mussels into a large pan with a cupful of water. Cover with a tight-fitting lid and quickly bring to the boil. Cook for about 5 minutes, shaking the pan occasionally, until the mussels have opened. Transfer them to a bowl with a slotted spoon, discarding any unopened ones; set aside.

3. Cut the squid pouches into thick rings. Cut the heads off the tentacles; leave the tentacles whole. Slice the sole or red mullet fillets into thick strips. Peel the prawns, leaving the tail end attached if desired. Using a small sharp knife, make a shallow slit along the back of each prawn and remove the dark intestinal vein. Dry all the seafood well on kitchen paper.

4. Heat the oil in a deep-fryer to 180°C (350°F) or until a crumb dropped into it sizzles instantly. Drop the squid into the batter and remove with a slotted spoon. Slip into the hot oil and fry for 2-3 minutes until golden and crisp. Remove with a slotted spoon and drain on kitchen paper. Keep warm in the low oven with the door ajar.

5. Repeat the procedure with the rest of the fish and shellfish in turn. Fry the sole or red mullet strips for 3 minutes; the prawns for 5 minutes; the whitebait for 3-4 minutes; the mussels for 2-3 minutes; drain and keep warm as above.

6. Toss all the cooked seafood together and sprinkle with salt. Transfer to a heated serving platter and serve immediately, with the lemon wedges.

NOTE: For convenience, you can use a bag of frozen seafood salad, thawed, drained and dried, supplemented by sole and red mullet.

VARIATION

For a simple version, toss all the seafood in plain white flour, shaking off excess, and deep-fry until golden and crisp.

TECHNIQUE

Using a slotted spoon, dip the squid into the batter, then deep-fry in the oil until golden and crisp. Drain on kitchen paper.

MARINATED PEPPERS WITH ARTICHOKES AND ANCHOVIES

There is nothing more evocative of sunny, warm Mediterranean meals than sweet roasted red peppers marinated in golden, garlicky olive oil with artichoke hearts and anchovies to add extra bite. Left overnight for the flavours to mature, the peppers release a sweet juice into the oil, making a delicious sauce – perfect for mopping up with copious amounts of bread.

SERVES 6

6 red, orange or yellow peppers (or a mixture)
12 artichoke hearts in oil, drained
24 salted anchovies (see below), or canned anchovy fillets
salt and pepper
4 garlic cloves
30 ml (2 tbsp) chopped fresh oregano
extra-virgin olive oil, for marinating

PREPARATION TIME
20 minutes, plus overnight marinating
COOKING TIME
10-15 minutes
FREEZING
Not suitable

300 CALS PER SERVING

1. Preheat the grill to high. Place the whole peppers in the grill pan and grill, turning occasionally, until the skins are evenly charred all over. Place in a covered bowl for 1-2 minutes until cool enough to handle.

2. Slip off the skins while the peppers are still warm, then cut in half lengthways and scrape out the seeds. Place the peppers cut-side up in a shallow dish.

3. Cut the artichoke hearts in half and place two halves in each pepper half. Lay the anchovy fillets on top. Season well with salt and pepper. Peel and slice the garlic. Scatter the garlic and chopped oregano over the peppers.

4. Pour over enough olive oil to cover the peppers (see note). Cover the dish and leave to marinate in the refrigerator overnight to permit the flavours to blend. Allow to come to room temperature before serving, with crusty Italian bread.

NOTE: Use the leftover flavoured olive oil again and again to make more of the same dish, or in salad dressings.

SALTED ANCHOVIES: These have a much better flavour than canned anchovy fillets. They are available in jars from Italian delicatessens and larger supermarkets. Usually salted anchovies are whole and have to be rinsed, split open and the backbone and other small bones removed.

VARIATION

Fill the peppers with grilled thin lengthwise slices of courgette and top with cubed mozzarella cheese.

TECHNIQUE

Place two artichoke halves in each grilled pepper half. Top with the anchovy fillets.

GRILLED PROSCIUTTO WITH FIGS

This is a truly summery dish to make when figs are plump and sweet, and barbecues are lit. The searing heat of the barbecue frazzles the Parma ham but leaves it still juicy, while the figs are roasted until warm and caramelised. If it's not the time for a barbecue, try using a ridged griddle, but it must be very hot!

SERVES 4

8 fresh ripe figs
olive oil, for basting
12 thin slices of Parma ham
   or other prosciutto (see
   note)
TO SERVE
extra-virgin olive oil
crushed black pepper
small chunks of Parmesan
   cheese

PREPARATION TIME
5 minutes
COOKING TIME
5-10 minutes
FREEZING
Not suitable

275 CALS PER SERVING

1. Stand each fig upright. Using a sharp knife, cut crosswise leaving the base of each fig intact. Ease the figs open and brush with olive oil.

2. Place the figs, cut-side down, on the barbecue or griddle and cook for 5-10 minutes until hot and golden brown, turning once. Alternatively, place under a preheated searing hot grill and grill until browning and hot through.

3. While the figs are cooking, place half the slices of Parma ham on the barbecue or griddle and cook for 2-3 minutes until frazzled and starting to crisp. Remove and keep warm while cooking the remaining Parma ham. (Alternatively use a very hot grill.)

4. Arrange 3 slices of Parma ham and 2 figs on each warmed serving plate. Drizzle with extra-virgin olive oil and season with plenty of crushed black pepper. Place a small chunk of fresh Parmesan on each plate.

NOTE: *Prosciutto crudo* is the generic term for cured raw ham. Parma ham, from the region of Parma, is arguably the best variety. Other types of prosciutto are produced in different parts of Italy.

VARIATION

Replace the figs with 2 peaches, halved and stoned. Cook cut-side down on the barbecue, then turn and cook the other side. Serve one peach half per person.

TECHNIQUE

Stand each fig upright on a board. Using a sharp knife, cut crosswise, leaving the base intact. Ease the figs open.

TOMATO AND MOZZARELLA SALAD ON BRUSCHETTA

A classic mozzarella and cherry tomato salad, which is marinated in olive oil, then piled onto garlic-scented toasted country bread and served surrounded with rocket and basil leaves. Bruschetta (pronounced *bruce-ketta*) is a popular snack all over Italy, served in bars and at home. The best bruschetta is toasted on the barbecue or over a wood fire, rubbed with garlic and drizzled with olive oil. The toppings are infinite – the simplest being a perfectly ripe tomato crushed onto the toast. Serve as a substantial starter, snack or lunch.

SERVES 4

12 boconcini (baby
    mozzarelle) or 375 g
    (12 oz) mozzarella
20 cherry tomatoes
45 ml (3 tbsp) olive oil
5 ml (1 tsp) balsamic or
    sherry vinegar
salt and pepper
4 thick slices of Italian
    country bread
2 garlic cloves, peeled
125 g (4 oz) rocket or
    watercress
extra olive oil, to serve
a generous handful of basil
    leaves, to garnish

PREPARATION TIME
15 minutes
COOKING TIME
Nil
FREEZING
Not suitable

590 CALS PER SERVING

1. Cut baby mozzarelle in half, or cut whole mozzarella into large cubes; place in a bowl. Halve the cherry tomatoes and add to the cheese.

2. Whisk together the olive oil and balsamic vinegar. Season with salt and pepper, then pour over the cheese and tomatoes. Stir well.

3. Preheat the grill and toast the slices of bread until golden on both sides. Halve the garlic cloves and rub over each slice of hot toasted bread.

4. Place a slice of toast on each serving plate and surround with the rocket. Pile the mozzarella and tomato mixture on the toast and drizzle the olive oil over the rocket. Garnish with basil leaves and serve at once.

NOTE: Baby mozzarelle are sold in tubs, immersed in water. They look very pretty in this salad, but ordinary mozzarella will do. Try to buy the round-shaped cheese, or even the expensive *mozzarella di bufala* (made with water-buffalo milk); these are superior in flavour and texture to the mozzarella bricks which are best used for pizzas.

VARIATION

Replace the mozzarella with chopped avocado.

TECHNIQUE

Rub the garlic cloves all over the hot toast to impart flavour.

SPAGHETTI WITH MUSSELS

This simple dish, spiced with chilli and garlic, relies heavily on the quality of the tomatoes used. The plump mussels and fragrant basil marry well with the intense flavour of the reduced wine and tomato sauce. There is not a lot of sauce – any more would overpower the mussels.

SERVES 4

900 g (2 lb) fresh mussels in shells

900 g (2 lb) really ripe fresh tomatoes

1 onion

4 garlic cloves, peeled

6 basil leaves

150 ml (¼ pint) white wine

2 red chillies

30 ml (2 tbsp) olive oil

salt and pepper

450 g (1 lb) dried spaghetti

small basil leaves, to garnish

PREPARATION TIME
20 minutes
COOKING TIME
35 minutes
FREEZING
Not suitable

575 CALS PER SERVING

1. Scrub the mussels thoroughly under cold running water and pull off the hairy 'beard' that protrudes from the shell. Discard any mussels with cracked or broken shells, and those that do not close when sharply tapped with the back of a knife.

2. Put the mussels into a large pan with a cupful of water. Cover with a tight-fitting lid and quickly bring to the boil. Cook for about 5 minutes, shaking the pan occasionally, until the mussels have opened. Transfer them to a bowl with a slotted spoon, discarding any unopened ones; set aside.

3. Strain the cooking juices through a muslin-lined sieve to remove any sand or grit; reserve.

4. Quarter the tomatoes and place them in a shallow saucepan. Peel and chop the onion; crush two of the garlic cloves. Add the onion and crushed garlic to the tomatoes with the basil. Bring to the boil and simmer for about 20 minutes until the tomatoes are beginning to disintegrate.

5. Press the tomato sauce through a nylon sieve or mouli to remove the seeds and skins. Return to the rinsed-out pan and pour in the reserved mussel liquid and wine. Bring to the boil and boil rapidly for 5 minutes or until reduced by about half.

6. Chop the other 2 garlic cloves; halve, deseed and chop the chillies. Heat the oil in another pan, add the garlic and chillies and cook until golden. Stir in the tomato sauce and mussels. Cover and simmer for 2-3 minutes until well heated through. Season with salt and pepper to taste.

7. Bring a large pan of salted water to the boil and add the spaghetti. Cook at a fast boil until *al dente*, tender but firm to the bite. Drain, holding back 30 ml (2 tbsp) cooking liquid – this will help the sauce to cling to the pasta. Stir in the mussel sauce. Pile into a large warmed serving dish and sprinkle with basil leaves. Serve immediately.

NOTE: If you prefer not to have the shells in the dish, remove the cooked mussels from their shells in stage 2, when they are cool enough to handle.

TECHNIQUE

Strain the mussel cooking liquor through a muslin-lined sieve to remove any sand or grit.

SPINACH AND RICOTTA RAVIOLI

A delicate filling of spinach and snowy white ricotta cheese, seasoned with nutmeg and pepper, is enveloped by fresh egg pasta and served tossed in melted butter. Slivers of freshly pared Parmesan complete this simple but delicious dish.

SERVES 4–6

PASTA
400 g (14 oz) plain white
   flour
salt
4 (size 2) eggs, beaten
15 ml (1 tbsp) olive oil
FILLING
450 g (1 lb) frozen spinach,
   thawed and squeezed dry
175 g (6 oz) fresh ricotta or
   curd cheese
2.5 ml ($\frac{1}{2}$ tsp) freshly grated
   nutmeg
5 ml (1 tsp) salt
pepper, to taste
TO FINISH
beaten egg, to seal
75 g (3 oz) butter, melted
25 g (1 oz) freshly pared
   Parmesan cheese

PREPARATION TIME
20 minutes, plus resting
COOKING TIME
3 minutes
FREEZING
Suitable: Stage 6

765–505 CALS PER SERVING

1. To make the pasta, sift the flour and a pinch of salt onto a clean work surface and make a well in the centre with your fist. Pour the beaten eggs and oil into the well. Gradually mix the eggs into the flour, using the fingers of one hand.

2. Knead the pasta until smooth, wrap in cling film and rest for at least 30 minutes before rolling out. The pasta will be much more elastic after resting.

3. To make the filling, place all the ingredients in a food processor or blender and process until smooth. Cover and refrigerate.

4. Cut the dough in half and re-wrap one piece in cling film. Roll the other piece out thinly on a lightly floured surface to a rectangle. Cover with a clean damp tea-towel and repeat with the remaining pasta.

5. Spoon or pipe small mounds, about 5 ml (1 tsp), of filling in even rows across one piece of the dough, spacing them at 4 cm (1½ inch) intervals. Brush the spaces of dough between the mounds with beaten egg. Using a rolling pin, carefully lift the other sheet of pasta over the top. Press down firmly between the pockets of filling, pushing out any trapped air.

6. Cut into squares, using a serrated ravioli cutter or sharp knife. Transfer to a floured tea-towel and leave to rest for 1 hour before cooking.

7. Bring a large saucepan of salted water to the boil. Add the ravioli and cook for about 3 minutes, until puffy. Drain well and toss with the melted butter. Serve topped with slivers of Parmesan.

VARIATION

For the filling, sauté 125 g (4 oz) chopped pancetta or thick-cut unsmoked bacon in butter until golden and crisp. Stir in 45 ml (3 tbsp) chopped fresh sage. Allow to cool, then beat into the ricotta filling. Continue as above.

TECHNIQUE

Brush the pasta dough between the small mounds of filling with beaten egg, to help seal the ravioli.

OLIVE TAGLIATELLE WITH PESTO TRAPANESE

This Sicilian pesto of garlic, basil, almonds, tomatoes and olive oil will complement any fresh or dried pasta. It's really a taste from the past which is very much in keeping with today's cooking. Pesto Trapanese goes beautifully with the homemade olive pasta.

SERVES 4

OLIVE PASTA
350 g (12 oz) plain white flour
salt
3 (size 2) eggs
45 ml (3 tbsp) black olive paste
PESTO TRAPANESE
3 ripe tomatoes
4 garlic cloves, peeled
salt and pepper
50 g (2 oz) fresh basil leaves
125 g (4 oz) blanched almonds
150 ml (¼ pint) olive oil
TO GARNISH
basil leaves

PREPARATION TIME
20 minutes, plus resting
COOKING TIME
2-3 minutes
FREEZING
Not suitable

565 CALS PER SERVING

1. To make the pasta, sift the flour and a pinch of salt onto a clean work surface and make a well in the centre with your fist. In a bowl, beat the eggs together with the olive paste, then pour into the well. Gradually mix the eggs into the flour, using the fingers of one hand.

2. Knead the pasta until smooth. The dough should be quite firm; add a little extra flour if it feels too soft. Wrap in cling film and allow to rest for at least 30 minutes before attempting to roll out. The pasta will be much more elastic after resting.

3. Meanwhile make the pesto. Place all the ingredients in a food processor or blender and blend until smooth. Transfer to a bowl and set aside (see note).

4. Roll out the pasta as thinly as possible, using a pasta machine if you have one. Dust with flour and roll up like a sausage. Using a sharp knife cut the pasta into 1 cm (½ inch) strips; unravel and place on a floured tea-towel until ready to cook. Alternatively, fit the tagliatelle cutters to your pasta machine and pass the pasta through.

5. Bring a large pan of boiling salted water to the boil. Add the pasta and cook for 2–3 minutes until *al dente*,

tender but firm to the bite. Drain well and toss with half of the pesto. Serve immediately, garnished with basil leaves.

NOTE: For this recipe, you will only need to use half of the pesto; it isn't practical to make a smaller quantity. Spoon the rest into a jar, cover with a layer of olive oil, and seal. Store in the refrigerator for up to 1 week.

VARIATION

Serve the pesto with plain egg pasta (see page 7) rather than olive pasta.

TECHNIQUE

Unravel the cut pasta and lay on a floured tea-towel until ready to cook.

MOZZARELLA-STUFFED RICE BALLS

These delicious crisp golden balls, stuffed with melting mozzarella and basil leaves are a good way to use up leftover risotto, but worth making from scratch too. Shaped into orange-sized balls, as below, they are a substantial snack. Alternatively as tiny bite-sized morsels, they are ideal finger food to serve with drinks.

SERVES 4

RISOTTO
1 red onion
75 g (3 oz) butter
150 ml (¼ pint) dry white wine
275 g (10 oz) arborio rice (Italian risotto rice)
1 litre (1¾ pints) chicken stock
salt and pepper
25 g (1 oz) freshly grated Parmesan cheese
TO FINISH
2 eggs
125 g (4 oz) mozzarella cheese
about 16 small basil leaves
125 g (4 oz) dried white breadcrumbs
oil for deep-frying

PREPARATION TIME
45 minutes
COOKING TIME
About 10-15 minutes
FREEZING
Not suitable

765 CALS PER SERVING

1. To make the risotto, peel and finely chop the onion. Melt the butter in a large saucepan, add the onion and fry gently for 5 minutes or until soft but not coloured. Pour in the wine and boil rapidly until almost totally reduced.

2. Add the rice and stir to coat with the butter and wine. Add a ladleful of stock and simmer, stirring, until absorbed. Continue adding the stock ladle by ladle until the rice is tender and creamy but still has some bite to it; this should take about 20 minutes. Make sure each addition of stock is absorbed before adding the next. (You may not need to use all of the stock.) Season generously with salt and pepper to taste and stir in the Parmesan. Allow to cool completely.

3. Beat the eggs together, then beat into the cold risotto. Cut the mozzarella into small cubes.

4. With moistened hands, take 15 ml (1 tbsp) risotto and spread in the palm of one hand. Lay a small basil leaf and a cube of mozzarella in the middle. Take another 15 ml (1 tbsp) of risotto and place over the mozzarella and basil to completely enclose. Shape to form a smooth round ball. Repeat until all the risotto is used up, to make about 16 rice balls in total.

5. Spread the breadcrumbs in a shallow dish. Roll the rice balls in the breadcrumbs until evenly covered.

6. Heat the oil in a deep-fryer to 180°C (350°F) or until a crumb dropped into the hot oil sizzles immediately. Fry the rice balls, a few at a time, for 3-5 minutes until golden and crisp. Drain on kitchen paper, sprinkle with salt and keep hot while cooking the remainder. Serve immediately.

NOTE: The rice balls can be prepared up to 8 hours ahead – to the end of stage 4. Keep covered in the refrigerator.

TECHNIQUE

Spread 15 ml (1 tbsp) risotto in your moistened palm, then place a basil leaf and a mozzarella cube on top. Cover with another 15 ml (1 tbsp) risotto and form into a ball.

POTATO GNOCCHI WITH RED PESTO

Classic potato gnocchi originate from Northern Italy, where they are a staple food. Here they're tossed with a red pesto made from basil, toasted pine nuts, sun-dried tomatoes, fresh tomatoes, chilli and roasted red peppers. It takes a little practice to make gnocchi really light – overworking makes them tough.

SERVES 4

PESTO
I large red pepper
50 g (2 oz) fresh basil leaves
I garlic clove, crushed
30 ml (2 tbsp) toasted pine
  nuts
6 sun-dried tomatoes in oil,
  drained
2 ripe tomatoes, skinned
45 ml (3 tbsp) tomato purée
2.5 ml (½ tsp) chilli powder
50 g (2 oz) freshly grated
  Parmesan cheese
150 ml (¼ pint) olive oil
GNOCCHI
900 g (2 lb) floury potatoes
salt
50 g (2 oz) butter
I egg, beaten
225-275 g (8-10 oz) plain
  white flour
TO GARNISH
basil leaves

PREPARATION TIME
30 minutes
COOKING TIME
20-30 minutes, plus 3 minutes
FREEZING
Not suitable

980– 655 CALS PER SERVING

1. Preheat the grill to high. Place the pepper on the grill rack and grill, turning occasionally, until blackened all over. Place in a covered bowl until cool enough to handle, then peel off the skin. Halve the pepper and remove the core and seeds. Place in a blender or food processor with the remaining pesto ingredients except the oil. Blend until smooth, then with the machine running, slowly add the oil.

2. To make the gnocchi, cook the unpeeled potatoes in boiling water for 20-30 minutes until very tender; drain well. Halve and press through a potato ricer, or peel and press through a sieve into a bowl.

3. While still warm, add 5 ml (I tsp) salt, the butter, beaten egg and half the flour. Lightly mix together, then turn out onto a floured board. Gradually knead in enough of the remaining flour to yield a smooth, soft, slightly sticky dough.

4. Roll the dough into thick sausages, 2.5 cm (I inch) in diameter. Cut into 2 cm (¾ inch) pieces and shape (see technique). Lay on a floured tea-towel.

5. Bring a large pan of salted water to the boil. Cook the gnocchi in batches. Drop them into the boiling water and

cook for 2-3 minutes, until they float to the surface. Remove with a slotted spoon and keep hot while cooking the remainder. Toss with the red pesto and serve immediately, garnished with basil.

NOTE: The red pesto can be stored in a jar, covered with a layer of oil, for up to 2 weeks in the refrigerator.

VARIATION

Serve the gnocchi with a classic pesto. Use 50 g (2 oz) fresh basil leaves; I garlic clove, crushed; 45 ml (3 tbsp) freshly grated Parmesan cheese; 25 g (I oz) pine nuts; 90 ml (6 tbsp) olive oil; pepper to taste. Process all the ingredients, except the oil, then add the oil as above.

TECHNIQUE

Roll each piece over the back of a fork with your floured thumb, to form ridges on one side and an indentation on the other.

FOCACCIA

This light multi-purpose bread is used to make sandwiches, and eaten as an accompaniment to soups, stews and hearty dishes throughout Italy. The secret of a truly light focaccia lies in three risings, and dimpling the dough so that it traps olive oil as it bakes; spraying the dough with water helps to keep the bread moist. You can create infinite toppings, and focaccia can be thin and crisp, or thick and soft, as you like!

MAKES 2
EACH SERVES 6-8

25 g (1 oz) fresh yeast, 15 ml
   (1 tbsp) dried active
   baking yeast, or 1 sachet
   easy-blend yeast
pinch of sugar
450 ml (¾ pint) warm water
700 g (1½ lb) strong plain
   white flour
105 ml (7 tbsp) extra-virgin
   olive oil
coarse sea or crystal salt, for
   sprinkling

PREPARATION TIME
30 minutes, plus rising
COOKING TIME
20-25 minutes
FREEZING
Suitable

275-210 CALS PER SERVING

1. In a bowl, cream the fresh yeast with the sugar and whisk in the warm water. Leave for 10 minutes until frothy. For other yeasts, use according to the manufacturer's instructions.

2. Sift the flour into a large bowl and make a well in the centre. Pour in the yeast mixture and 45 ml (3 tbsp) olive oil. Mix together with a round-bladed knife, then using your hands until the dough comes together.

3. With clean, dry hands, knead dough on a floured surface for 10 minutes until smooth, elastic and quite soft. If too soft to handle, knead in a little more flour.

4. Place in a clean oiled bowl, cover with a damp tea towel and leave to rise for about 1½ hours until doubled in size.

5. Lightly oil two shallow 25 cm (10 inch) metal pizza or pie plates. Knock back the dough and divide in half. Shape each piece into a round ball on a floured surface and roll out to a 25 cm (10 inch) circle. Place in the oiled tins. Cover with a damp tea-towel and leave to rise for 30 minutes.

6. Remove the tea-towel and, using your fingertips, make deep dimples all over the surface of the dough. Cover and leave to rise once more until doubled in size – about 2 hours.

7. Drizzle over the remaining oil and sprinkle generously with salt. Spray with water and bake at 200°C (400°F) Mark 6 for 20-25 minutes. Spray with water twice during cooking. Transfer to a wire rack to cool. Eat the same day or freeze as soon as it is cool.

VARIATIONS

Olive and Sun-dried Tomato Focaccia: Drain 50 g (2 oz) sun-dried tomatoes in oil, slice and knead into the dough at stage 3. Sprinkle the dough with 225 g (8 oz) black or green olives at stage 7.

Sage and Onion Focaccia: Chop 20 sage leaves. Peel and thinly slice 2 small red onions. Knead the chopped sage into the dough at stage 3. Sprinkle the dough with extra sage leaves and the onion slices at stage 7.

TECHNIQUE

Using your fingertips, make deep dimples all over the surface of the dough.

TOMATO, ARTICHOKE AND PROSCIUTTO PIZZA

A large sumptuous crisp pizza topped with chunky vegetables and sweet prosciutto which cooks to a delicious crispness. The artichokes and plum tomatoes give the pizza juiciness, the latter keeping their shape in the short cooking time.

SERVES 4

PIZZA DOUGH
15 g (½ oz) fresh yeast,
    15 ml (1 tbsp) dried active
    baking yeast, or 1 sachet
    easy-blend yeast
pinch of sugar
250 ml (8 fl oz) warm water
350 g (12 oz) strong plain
    white flour
30 ml (2 tbsp) olive oil
2.5 ml (½ tsp) salt
TOPPING
4 ripe plum tomatoes
8 artichoke hearts in oil,
    drained
4 large garlic cloves
150 g (5 oz) mozzarella
    cheese
45 ml (3 tbsp) sun-dried
    tomato paste
6 slices prosciutto
olive oil, for drizzling
45 ml (3 tbsp) freshly grated
    Parmesan cheese
TO GARNISH
oregano or basil leaves

PREPARATION TIME
30 minutes, plus rising
COOKING TIME 15-20 minutes
FREEZING Not suitable

665 CALS PER SERVING

1. To make the pizza dough, in a bowl, cream the fresh yeast with the sugar, then whisk in the warm water. Leave for 10 minutes until frothy. For other yeasts, use according to the manufacturer's instructions.

2. Sift the flour into a large bowl and make a well in the centre. Pour in the yeast mixture, olive oil and salt. Mix together with a round-bladed knife, then using your hands until the dough comes together.

3. Tip out onto a floured surface. With clean, dry hands, knead the dough for 10 minutes until smooth, elastic and quite soft. If too soft to handle, knead in a little more flour.

4. Place in a clean oiled bowl, cover with a damp tea-towel and leave to rise for about 1 hour until doubled in size.

5. Cut each tomato into six wedges. Halve or quarter the artichoke hearts. Peel and finely slice the garlic. Slice the mozzarella.

6. Preheat the oven to 230°C (450°F) Mark 8. Knock back the dough and roll out, or stretch with your fingers, to a 30 cm (12 inch) circle on a large floured baking sheet.

7. Spread the sun-dried tomato paste over the pizza base. Arrange half the mozzarella slices on the base. Scatter over the tomatoes, artichoke hearts and garlic. Scrunch up the prosciutto and drape over the pizza. Scatter over the remaining mozzarella and drizzle with oil. Sprinkle with the Parmesan. Bake for 15-20 minutes until golden and sizzling. Serve immediately, sprinkled with oregano or basil leaves.

NOTE: To make two smaller pizzas, halve the dough and roll out two 20 cm (8 inch) circles.

VARIATION

For a vegetarian pizza, replace the ham with grilled aubergine slices.

TECHNIQUE

Scrunch up the prosciutto slices and drape over the pizza.

WHITE ONION PIZZA

This succulent golden pizza is the forerunner of the French *pissaladière*. The onions are cooked in olive oil to a creamy softness, then spread onto the pizza base before baking. Add more herbs if you like – dried herbs work well in this pizza. If you hate anchovies, leave them out, but they do add a delicious savoury saltiness to the sweet onions!

SERVES 4

PIZZA DOUGH
15 g (½ oz) fresh yeast,
   15 ml (1 tbsp) dried active
   baking yeast, or 1 sachet
   easy-blend yeast
pinch of sugar
250 ml (8 fl oz) warm water
350 g (12 oz) strong plain
   white flour
30 ml (2 tbsp) olive oil
2.5 ml (½ tsp) salt
TOPPING
900 g (2 lb) onions
100 ml (3½ fl oz) olive oil
15 ml (1 tbsp) chopped fresh
   oregano
15 ml (1 tbsp) chopped fresh
   rosemary
12 anchovy fillets in oil,
   drained
16 black olives, stoned
TO GARNISH
rosemary sprigs
oregano leaves

PREPARATION TIME
30 minutes, plus rising
COOKING TIME
40 minutes–1 hour for onions,
plus 15 minutes baking
FREEZING
Not suitable

705 CALS PER SERVING

1. To make the pizza dough, in a bowl, cream the fresh yeast with the sugar, then whisk in the warm water. Leave for 10 minutes until frothy. For other yeasts, use according to manufacturer's instructions.

2. Sift the flour into a large bowl and make a well in the centre. Pour in the yeast mixture, olive oil and salt. Mix together with a round-bladed knife, then using your hands until the dough comes together.

3. Tip out onto a floured surface. With clean, dry hands, knead the dough for 10 minutes until smooth, elastic and quite soft. If too soft to handle, knead in a little more flour.

4. Place in a clean oiled bowl, cover with a damp-tea towel and leave to rise for about 1 hour until doubled in size.

5. Meanwhile, peel and finely slice the onions. Heat the oil in a heavy-based saucepan. Add the onions and cook over a gentle heat, stirring occasionally, for 40 minutes to 1 hour until they are completely soft and golden; they must not brown. Stir in the chopped herbs.

6. Preheat the oven to 230°C (450°F) Mark 8. Knock back the dough and roll out, or stretch with your fingers, to a 30 cm (12 inch) circle on a large floured baking sheet.

7. Spoon the onions on top of the pizza and spread evenly. Scatter over the anchovy fillets and olives. Bake for 15 minutes until golden and crisp. Scatter over the rosemary sprigs and oregano leaves. Serve immediately.

NOTE: To make two smaller pizzas, halve the dough and roll out two 20 cm (8 inch) circles.

VARIATION

Cover the base with sliced mozzarella before spreading with the onions. Sprinkle with 30 ml (2 tbsp) freshly grated Parmesan cheese.

TECHNIQUE

Stretch the pizza dough with your fingers to a 30 cm (12 inch) circle on a large floured baking sheet.

STUFFED SARDINES

Fresh sardines are easily boned with the flick of a finger. Here they are opened out and stuffed with a sweet and savoury mixture of pine nuts, parsley and raisins, then rolled and baked until tender. A tomato and onion salad is the perfect accompaniment.

SERVES 4

16 fresh sardines

50 g (2 oz) pine nuts, toasted

50 g (2 oz) raisins

45 ml (3 tbsp) chopped fresh parsley

finely grated rind and juice of 1 orange

salt and pepper

100 ml (3½ fl oz) olive oil

PREPARATION TIME
25 minutes
COOKING TIME
10 minutes
FREEZING
Not suitable

365 CALS PER SERVING

1. Preheat the oven to 180°C (350°F) Mark 4. Scrape the scales from the sardines if necessary, then cut off the heads. Slit open the bellies and clean the insides under cold running water. Lay, flesh-side down, on a board. Slide your thumb along the backbone, pressing firmly to release the flesh along its length. Take hold of the backbone at the head end and lift it out; the fish should now be open like a book.

2. For the stuffing, mix together the pine nuts, raisins, parsley, orange rind, and salt and pepper to taste. Place a spoonful of stuffing on the flesh side of each fish. Roll up from the head end and secure with a cocktail stick if necessary.

3. Place the stuffed sardines in an oiled ovenproof dish into which they fit snugly. It is important that the sardines are tightly packed together. Tuck in a few bay leaves here and there. Pour over the orange juice and olive oil. Season with salt and pepper and bake for about 10 minutes. Serve hot or cold, with a tomato and onion salad.

NOTE: The cooking time will vary depending on the type of baking dish used. The sardines will cook more quickly in a thin metal baking tin than in a terracotta baking dish, for example. Avoid using frozen sardines as they have a disappointing flavour.

VARIATION

Use fresh sprats instead of sardines.

TECHNIQUE

To release the backbone from the flesh, lay the sardine, flesh side down, and press firmly along the backbone with your thumb.

CHAR-GRILLED SQUID WITH CHILLIES AND AUBERGINES

Baby squid are marinated in chilli, garlic and olive oil, then char-grilled to a smoky sweetness and served on a bed of rocket and grilled aubergine. These soak up the spicy juices and cut through the richness. For best results use a searing hot griddle. If you do not have a griddle, use the grill – at its highest setting.

SERVES 4

700 g (1½ lb) baby squid
2 garlic cloves
2 small red chillies
60 ml (4 tbsp) olive oil
juice of 1 lemon
5 ml (1 tsp) chilli sauce
2 medium aubergines
salt and pepper
vegetable oil, for basting
TO SERVE
rocket leaves
lemon wedges

PREPARATION TIME
15 minutes, plus marinating
COOKING TIME
15 minutes
FREEZING
Not suitable

380 CALS PER SERVING

1. To prepare the squid, rinse well. Hold the body in one hand and firmly pull the tentacles with the other, to remove the soft contents of the body pouch. Cut the tentacles just in front of the eyes and discard the body contents, reserve the tentacles. Rinse the body pouches under cold running water.

2. Peel and finely chop the garlic; halve, deseed and chop the chillies. Place in a shallow dish with the olive oil, lemon juice and chilli sauce. Add the squid pouches and tentacles, stir well, cover and leave to marinate for 2 hours.

3. Meanwhile, slice the aubergine thinly. Spread the aubergine slices in a colander and sprinkle with salt. Leave to degorge for 20 minutes. Rinse well and pat dry with kitchen paper.

4. Heat a griddle until smoking and brush with oil. (Alternatively preheat the grill to high and brush the aubergine slices with oil.) Cook the aubergine slices in batches for 2 minutes on each side. Keep warm in a low oven.

5. Remove the squid from the marinade using a slotted spoon, reserving the marinade. Heat the griddle once more and cook (or grill) the squid pouches for 2 minutes on each side. Transfer the squid pouches to a warmed dish; keep hot. Add the squid tentacles to the griddle (or grill) and cook for 1-2 minutes. Pour the marinade into a pan and heat gently.

6. Arrange the aubergine slices on warmed serving plates. Pile the squid on top and spoon over a little marinade. Surround with a few rocket leaves. Serve immediately, with lemon wedges.

NOTE: If baby squid are unobtainable, use large ones instead but slice the pouches into rings before cooking.

TECHNIQUE

To prepare the squid, cut the heads off the tentacles just below the eyes.

SEA BASS BAKED WITH FENNEL

This beautiful fish is baked on a bed of fennel, olives, lemon and herbs until tender and perfumed with their flavours. The fennel – which stays slightly crunchy – is the perfect foil for the sea bass. This is a great no-fuss dinner party dish.

SERVES 4

1 sea bass, about 1.1 kg
  (2½ lb), scaled and gutted
4 fresh rosemary sprigs
3 large fennel bulbs
60 ml (4 tbsp) olive oil
juice of 1 lemon
30 ml (2 tbsp) chopped fresh
  oregano
30 ml (2 tbsp) chopped fresh
  parsley
salt and pepper
150 ml (¼ pint) dry white
  wine
20 large green olives, stoned

PREPARATION TIME
20 minutes
COOKING TIME
30 minutes
FREEZING
Not suitable

405 CALS PER SERVING

1. Preheat the oven to 220°C (425°F) Mark 7. Wash the fish inside and out, then pat dry on kitchen paper. Lay in an oval ovenproof dish. Put the rosemary sprigs in the cavity of the fish.

2. Cut the fennel bulbs in half lengthwise, cut out the core and slice thickly.

3. In a medium bowl, whisk together the oil, lemon juice, chopped herbs and seasoning. Add the fennel slices and toss well. Spoon the fennel over and around the fish, pouring on any remaining marinade. Add the wine and scatter over the olives.

4. Bake for 30 minutes, stirring the fennel around and basting with the juices halfway through cooking. Turn off the oven but leave the fish inside for 5 minutes to set. Serve immediately, with Garlic Potatoes (see page 64).

NOTE: If you prefer the fennel to have a softer texture, first blanch the slices in boiling salted water for 2 minutes. Drain well and continue as above.

VARIATION

Use a small salmon in place of the sea bass. Replace the olives with chunks of cucumber.

TECHNIQUE

Rinse the sea bass thoroughly inside and out under cold running water. In particular, make sure it is cleaned very well close to the backbone.

SAFFRON SEAFOOD RISOTTO

A wonderful seafood and wine risotto, bright yellow and fragrant with saffron. The risotto takes a little time to make, but emerges deliciously creamy and packed with all manner of delights from the sea.

SERVES 6

2 sachets of saffron threads

350 g (12 oz) raw prawns in shell

1.4 litres (2½ pints) fish stock

300 ml (½ pint) dry white wine

6 baby squid, cleaned

6 fresh scallops, shelled

600 ml (1 pint) fresh mussels in shells

300 ml (½ pint) fresh venus clams in shells

1 onion

75 g (3 oz) butter

500 g (1 lb 2 oz) packet risotto rice

45 ml (3 tbsp) chopped fresh parsley

PREPARATION TIME
20 minutes
COOKING TIME
30 minutes
FREEZING
Not suitable

690 CALS PER SERVING

1. Place the saffron threads in a small bowl, cover with a little boiling water and leave to infuse.

2. Twist the heads off the prawns and put them in a saucepan with the stock and wine. Bring to the boil, cover and simmer for 10 minutes. Set aside the prawns.

3. Meanwhile, cut the squid pouches into rings and cut the tentacles from the heads, discarding the heads. Remove the hard white muscle from one side of each scallop, then separate the white meat from the orange roe. Scrub the mussels well and pull off any beards; discard any that do not close when sharply tapped. Scrub the clams, discarding any open ones.

4. Strain the stock into a clean pan and bring to simmering point. Add the prawns and cook for 2 minutes. Add the squid, white scallop meat and roe; cook for a further 2 minutes. Remove all these shellfish with a slotted spoon and set aside. Add the mussels and clams to the stock and bring to the boil. Cover with a tight-fitting lid and cook for 5 minutes or until the shellfish have opened. Remove with a slotted spoon and set aside. Discard any with unopened shells.

5. Meanwhile, peel and chop the onion. Melt the butter in a large saucepan, add the onion and cook gently for about 5 minutes until soft but not coloured.

Add the rice and stir to coat with the butter. Add the saffron and soaking water, plus a ladleful of the stock. Simmer, stirring until absorbed. Continue adding the stock, a ladleful at a time until only 2 ladlefuls remain, and the rice is tender but still has some bite to it. This should take about 20 minutes. Season generously with salt and pepper to taste.

6. Stir in the remaining stock with the seafood, cover and cook gently for 5 minutes or until piping hot. Transfer to a large warmed bowl and sprinkle with the parsley. Serve immediately.

VARIATION

Use ready-prepared frozen mixed seafood. Allow to thaw thoroughly, then add at stage 6, making sure the seafood is thoroughly heated through.

TECHNIQUE

Remove the tough white muscle from one side of each scallop, then separate the orange roe from the white meat.

CHICKEN AND WILD MUSHROOMS WITH RISOTTO

Golden chicken breasts, sautéed in butter and simmered in dry vermouth with wild mushrooms, are served with white risotto to mop up the delicious savoury juices. Italians are passionate collectors of wild mushrooms in the autumn. If you aren't fortunate enough to be able to collect or buy wild mushrooms, a selection of different cultivated ones – such as brown cap, shiitake and oyster mushrooms – works well. To enhance their flavour, include a handful of dried porcini (see variation).

SERVES 4

75 g (3 oz) butter

2 garlic cloves, crushed

4 boneless corn-fed chicken breasts

150 ml (¼ pint) dry white vermouth

salt and pepper

450 g (1 lb) mixed wild or cultivated mushrooms

30 ml (2 tbsp) chopped fresh oregano

RISOTTO

1 onion

75 g (3 oz) butter

150 ml (¼ pint) dry white wine

275 g (10 oz) arborio rice (Italian risotto rice)

1 litre (1¾ pints) chicken stock

salt and pepper

25 g (1 oz) freshly grated Parmesan cheese

PREPARATION TIME
20 minutes
COOKING TIME
30-40 minutes
FREEZING Not suitable

860 CALS PER SERVING

1. Melt 25 g (1 oz) of the butter in a sauté pan. When foaming, add the garlic and cook for 2 minutes until golden. Add the chicken breasts, skin-side down, and brown well on all sides. Don't let the butter burn.

2. Pour in the vermouth and season well with salt and pepper. Bring to the boil, cover and simmer for 30-40 minutes until the chicken is tender.

3. Meanwhile, halve or slice any large mushrooms and melt the remaining butter in another pan. When foaming, add the mushrooms and sauté for 3-5 minutes until cooked but still firm. Set aside.

4. To make the risotto, peel and finely chop the onion. Melt half the butter in a large saucepan, add the onion and cook gently for 5 minutes until soft but not coloured. Pour in the wine and boil rapidly until it has almost completely reduced.

5. Add the rice and stir to coat with the butter and wine. Add a ladleful of stock and simmer, stirring, until absorbed. Continue adding the stock, a ladleful at a time, until the rice is tender and creamy, but still has some bite to it. This should

take about 20 minutes; it may not be necessary to add all of the stock. Season well with salt and pepper and stir in the remaining butter and Parmesan.

6. Gently stir the mushrooms and any cooking juices into the chicken with the chopped oregano. Serve immediately, with the white risotto.

VARIATION

Soak 15 g (½ oz) dried porcini in hot water to cover for 20 minutes, then drain; strain and reserve the soaking liquid. Add the porcini with the fresh mushrooms. Use the soaking liquid in place of a little of the stock.

TECHNIQUE

Sauté the mushrooms in the butter for 3-5 minutes until cooked but still firm.

LEMON CHICKEN

Corn-fed chicken pieces are marinated in lemon juice, chilli and garlic, with a touch of honey — to help brown the chicken skin during cooking. Ripe, juicy lemon halves are tucked in and around the joints to impart extra flavour during roasting.

SERVES 4

1.6 kg (3½ lb) corn-fed or
   free-range chicken, or
   4 chicken joints
4 really ripe juicy lemons
8 garlic cloves
1-2 small red chillies
15 ml (1 tbsp) honey
60 ml (4 tbsp) chopped fresh
   parsley
salt and pepper

PREPARATION TIME
20 minutes, plus marinating
COOKING TIME
45 minutes
FREEZING
Suitable

190 CALS PER SERVING

1. Using a sharp knife and/or poultry shears, cut the whole chicken, if using, into 8 small or 4 large joints. Place the chicken joints, skin-side down, in a large shallow ovenproof baking dish.

2. Halve the lemons, squeeze the juice and pour into a small bowl; reserve the empty lemon halves.

3. Peel and crush two of the garlic cloves and add to the lemon juice. Halve the chilli(es) lengthwise and remove the seeds. Add to the lemon juice with the honey. Stir well, pour over the chicken and tuck the lemon halves around. Cover and leave to marinate for at least 2 hours, turning once or twice.

4. Preheat the oven to 200°C (400°F) Mark 6. Turn the chicken skin-side up. Halve the rest of the garlic cloves and scatter over the chicken. Roast in the oven for 45 minutes or until golden brown and tender. Stir in the parsley and season with salt and pepper to taste. Serve hot, garnished with the roasted lemon halves.

NOTE: This dish relies on the natural sweetness of really ripe lemons. Do not use under-ripe fruit.

VARIATION

● Spatchcocked poussins may be cooked in the same manner.
● Small oranges or tangerines can be used in place of lemons.

TECHNIQUE

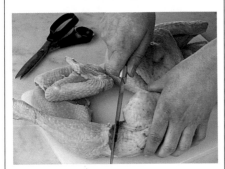

Using a sharp knife and/or poultry shears, cut the whole chicken into 8 small or 4 large joints.

PIGEON ON CRISP POLENTA

Italians are very fond of game — and game birds in particular. For this dish, which is typically Tuscan, crisp-fried slices of golden polenta are spread with chicken livers and garlic, then topped with rosy pink grilled pigeon breasts. The whole thing is served on a bed of fresh tomato sauce.

SERVES 4

4 wood pigeons, plucked and
    drawn
4 chicken livers
75 g (3 oz) butter
I garlic clove, crushed
pinch of powdered mace
POLENTA
175 g (6 oz) coarse polenta
30 ml (2 tbsp) chopped fresh
    sage
15 ml (1 tbsp) chopped fresh
    rosemary
salt and pepper
TOMATO SAUCE
4 large ripe tomatoes
2 garlic cloves
60 ml (4 tbsp) chopped fresh
    herbs, such as basil,
    marjoram, oregano or
    parsley, or a mixture
150 ml (¼ pint) olive oil
TO GARNISH
rosemary and sage sprigs

PREPARATION TIME
40 minutes, plus standing
COOKING TIME
25 minutes
FREEZING
Not suitable

790 CALS PER SERVING

I. First make the polenta. Bring 900 ml (1½ pints) water to the boil in a large saucepan with a good pinch of salt added. Sprinkle in the coarse polenta, whisking constantly. Lower the heat and simmer, stirring frequently, for 20 minutes or until the polenta leaves the side of the pan; it will be very thick. Stir in the herbs and plenty of salt and pepper. Turn out onto a wooden board and shape into a mound. Leave for about I hour to set, then cut 4 thick slices from it.

2. Meanwhile, make the tomato sauce. Immerse the tomatoes in boiling water for I minute, lift out with a slotted spoon and plunge into cold water. Peel off the skins, halve the tomatoes and squeeze out the seeds. Dice the flesh and place in a bowl. Peel and finely chop the garlic and add to the tomatoes with the herbs, oil, salt and pepper. Cover and set aside for at least 30 minutes.

3. Cut the legs from the pigeons and set aside. With a sharp knife, cut down the breast bone on each side and ease off the pigeon breasts. Cover and set aside.

4. Trim the chicken livers. Melt 25 g (1 oz) butter in a frying pan, add the garlic and fry for 2 minutes until golden. Stir in the chicken livers and cook over a high heat for 5 minutes until browned on the outside, but still pink in the middle. Season with the mace, salt and pepper. Transfer to a bowl.

5. Melt the remaining butter in the frying pan. When foaming, add the polenta slices and fry on both sides until golden; keep warm.

6. Preheat the grill. Brush the pigeon breasts and legs with oil. Lay the legs on the grill rack and grill for 2 minutes. Add the breasts, skin-side up, and grill for 4 minutes. Turn both legs and breasts over and grill for 2 minutes.

7. Meanwhile, heat the tomato sauce. Mash the chicken livers and spread on the fried polenta slices. Place on warmed serving plates and top with the pigeon. Garnish with sage and rosemary, and serve with the tomato sauce.

NOTE: For convenience you can use quick-cook polenta, following the manufacturer's instructions.

TECHNIQUE

Using a spatula, shape the polenta into a mound on a wooden board.

OSSO BUCCO WITH RISOTTO MILANESE

This easy Milanese dish of veal in a rich tomato sauce is perfect for a winter's dinner party and tastes even better if cooked the day before and reheated. Gremolata – an aromatic mixture of parsley, garlic and lemon rind – is always sprinkled over the finished dish and a saffron risotto is the classic accompaniment.

SERVES 4

4 thick slices shin of veal for 'osso bucco'
salt and pepper
flour, for coating
30 ml (2 tbsp) olive oil
150 ml (¼ pint) dry white wine
400 g (14 oz) can chopped tomatoes (see note)
about 450 ml (¾ pint) veal or chicken stock

GREMOLATA
1 garlic clove
60 ml (4 tbsp) chopped fresh parsley
15 ml (1 tbsp) finely grated lemon rind

RISOTTO
1 onion
50 g (2 oz) butter
150 ml (¼ pint) dry white wine
275 g (10 oz) arborio rice
1 packet saffron threads
1 litre (1¾ pints) veal or chicken stock
50 g (2 oz) freshly grated Parmesan cheese

PREPARATION TIME
20 minutes
COOKING TIME
About 2 hours

FREEZING Suitable: Stage 2

705 CALS PER SERVING

1. Dip the veal in seasoned flour to coat evenly, shaking off excess. Heat the oil in a flameproof casserole (into which the meat fits snugly in one layer). Add the meat and brown on all sides.

2. Stir in the wine and tomatoes. Bring to the boil and simmer, uncovered, for 10 minutes. Pour in enough stock to cover the meat and add seasoning. Cover tightly and simmer gently for 1¾-2 hours until the veal is very tender. (Alternatively bake in a preheated oven at 170°C (325° F) Mark 3.)

3. Check the sauce: it should be quite thick. If not, transfer the meat to a warmed dish; boil the sauce rapidly to reduce, then return the meat to the casserole.

4. Meanwhile, make the gremolata. Peel and crush the garlic and mix with the chopped parsley and lemon rind.

5. To make the risotto, peel and chop the onion. Melt half the butter in a large saucepan, add the onion and cook gently for 5 minutes until soft but not coloured. Pour in the wine and boil rapidly until almost totally reduced.

6. Add the rice and stir to coat with the butter. Add the saffron and a ladleful of stock and simmer, stirring, until absorbed. Continue adding the stock ladle by ladle until the rice is tender and creamy but still has some bite to it. This should take about 20 minutes; it may not be necessary to add all of the stock.

7. About 5 minutes before serving, sprinkle the gremolata over the meat. Stir the remaining butter and the Parmesan into the risotto and season with salt and pepper to taste. Serve immediately, with the Osso Bucco.

NOTE: When ripe flavourful tomatoes are available, use 450 g (1 lb), skinned and chopped, in place of the canned tomatoes.

TECHNIQUE

Add the stock a ladleful at a time, making sure each addition is absorbed before you add the next.

BEEF BRAISED IN BAROLO

In Piedmont, where dark full-bodied Barolo wine comes from, a whole piece of beef is marinated in Barolo, then slowly braised and served sliced with the puréed sauce. In this version, the wine is first boiled to concentrate the flavour and the meat is cut into large chunks. After the long, slow cooking the sauce is dark and luxurious. Serve with Garlic Potatoes (page 64) and a green vegetable.

SERVES 6-8

2 bottles Barolo wine
1.4 kg (3 lb) stewing beef, such as shin, chuck or skirt
2 onions
2 carrots
2 celery sticks
2 bay leaves
2 large fresh thyme sprigs
6 peppercorns
2 allspice berries, crushed
30 ml (2 tbsp) olive oil
30 ml (2 tbsp) tomato purée or sun-dried tomato paste
300-600 ml ($\frac{1}{2}$-1 pint) beef stock (approximately)
salt and pepper

PREPARATION TIME
30 minutes, plus overnight marinating
COOKING TIME
2-3 hours
FREEZING
Suitable

505-385 CALS PER SERVING

1. Pour the wine into a large saucepan or sauté pan. Bring to the boil and boil rapidly until reduced by half to 750 ml (1½ pints). Cool completely.

2. Trim the meat of any fat or gristle and cut into 6 cm (2½ inch) pieces. Peel and chop the vegetables. Place the meat and vegetables in a large polythene bag with the bay leaves, thyme sprigs, peppercorns and crushed allspice berries. Pour in the cold wine, shake to mix, then seal and leave to marinate in the refrigerator overnight.

3. Open the bag and pour the contents into a colander or sieve over a bowl. Separate the meat from the vegetables and pat dry.

4. Heat the oil in a large flameproof casserole and brown the meat in batches on all sides. Return all the meat to the casserole and stir in the vegetables, with the herbs and spices.

5. Pour over the reserved marinade and wine. Stir in the tomato purée, then add enough stock to just cover the meat and vegetables. Bring to the boil, lower the heat, cover tightly and simmer gently for 2-3 hours or until the meat is very tender. (Alternatively cook in a preheated oven at 170°C (325°F) Mark 3.) Top up the liquid with extra stock if it evaporates too quickly.

6. Using a slotted spoon, lift the meat out of the casserole and place in a bowl. Discard the bay leaves. Pour the sauce and vegetables into a blender or food processor and work until smooth. Adjust the seasoning. The sauce should be quite thick; if not, boil to reduce.

7. Stir the meat into the sauce and reheat until piping hot. Serve sprinkled with parsley.

VARIATION

Cook the meat whole, basting with the sauce every 30 minutes. Serve cut into thin slices, with the sauce.

TECHNIQUE

Put the meat and vegetables in a large polythene bag with the herbs and spices. Pour in the cold wine, shake to mix, then seal.

ITALIAN SAUSAGES

Real sausages – made with pure pork and highly seasoned with black pepper – are easy to make. Certain recipes call for Italian sausages, and these fit the bill if you haven't access to an Italian delicatessen. The secret lies in mincing or hand-chopping the meat coarsely, and using a proportion of gammon to give the right salty taste. The mixture can be filled into sausage skins, made into meatballs or patties, or used as sausagemeat.

SERVES 6

450 g (1 lb) shoulder of pork
225 g (8 oz) piece unsmoked
   gammon
225 g (8 oz) belly of pork
2 large garlic cloves, peeled
   (optional)
15 ml (1 tbsp) coarse sea
   salt
15 ml (1 tbsp) granulated
   sugar
30 ml (2 tbsp) coarsely
   crushed black pepper
sausage casings (optional)

PREPARATION TIME
45 minutes
COOKING TIME
10-15 minutes
FREEZING
Suitable: Up to 3 months

340 CALS PER SERVING

1. Trim the shoulder of pork, gammon and belly pork of any skin or connective tissue, then cut into rough chunks.

2. Pass through the coarse blade of a mincer or chop with a large sharp knife or cleaver (see note).

3. Place the meat in a large bowl. Crush the garlic, if using, and add to the meat with the sea salt, sugar and pepper. Mix thoroughly.

4. Shape the mixture into patties or roll into balls and dust with flour before cooking. Alternatively use to fill sausage casings as follows. Spoon the sausage-meat into a large piping bag fitted with a large plain plastic nozzle. Rinse the casings in cold water and roll the open end over the nozzle. Hold the first 5 cm (2 inches) casing closed and squeeze the filling into the casing to form the first sausage, easing the casing from the nozzle as it fills. Stop when the sausage is big enough and twist gently before filling the next one. Tie the loose end of the casing on the first sausage. Continue until all the filling is used up. If you like, tie the sausages at two points between the links with fine string, then cut into individual sausages.

5. To cook, heat a little oil in a frying pan and gently fry the sausages for 10-15 minutes, turning once or twice until cooked through. Alternatively cook under a preheated grill for 5 minutes on each side. Serve with fresh tomato sauce or grilled polenta.

NOTE: Large food mixers have a mincer attachment, and small hand-cranked ones are available. Do not use a food processor as this gives a poor texture.

Any good butcher who makes his own sausages should be able to supply sausage skins or casings.

VARIATIONS

Salsicce Genovese: Add 45 ml (3 tbsp) chopped fresh basil, 45 ml (3 tbsp) freshly grated Parmesan and 30 ml (2 tbsp) pine nuts to the mixture.
Salsicce Finocchio: Add 30 ml (2 tbsp) fennel seeds and 5 ml (1 tsp) dried chilli flakes to the meat mixture.

TECHNIQUE

With clean hands, mix all the sausage ingredients together thoroughly.

ITALIAN SAUSAGE RAGU WITH SOFT POLENTA

This winter-warmer comes from the north of Italy where polenta is a staple food. A thick, rich, spicy sausage and tomato sauce is served with soft polenta, as you would mashed potato. Bland golden polenta is the perfect foil for the hearty sauce. Buy the sausages fresh from an Italian delicatessen or – better still – make your own!

SERVES 4

450 g (1 lb) fresh Italian
   sausages (see page 54)
1 onion
30 ml (2 tbsp) olive oil
450 ml (¾ pint) passata
150 ml (¼ pint) dry red
   wine
6 sun-dried tomatoes in oil,
   drained
salt and pepper
300 g (10 oz) quick-cook
   polenta
freshly grated Parmesan
   cheese, to serve

PREPARATION TIME
15 minutes
COOKING TIME
30 minutes
FREEZING
Suitable

785 CALS PER SERVING

1. Put the sausagemeat into a bowl squeezing it out of the skins if necessary; break up the meat.

2. Peel and chop the onion. Heat the oil in a saucepan, add the onion and cook for 5 minutes until soft and golden. Add the sausagemeat and fry until evenly browned, stirring with a wooden spoon to break up the lumps. Pour in the passata and the wine. Bring to the boil.

3. Slice the sun-dried tomatoes and add to the sauce. Simmer, uncovered, for 30 minutes or until well reduced, stirring occasionally. Season with salt and pepper to taste.

4. Meanwhile, in a large saucepan bring 1.4 litres (2½ pints) water to the boil with 10 ml (2 tsp) salt added. Sprinkle in the polenta, stirring or whisking to prevent lumps forming. Simmer for 5-10 minutes, stirring constantly, until thickened like soft mashed potato.

5. Spoon the polenta into 4 warmed large soup plates and make a shallow dip in the centre of each. Top with the sausage ragù and serve with grated Parmesan cheese.

NOTE: As an alternative to fresh Italian sausages, you could use good butcher's sausages mixed with a little crushed garlic, lots of freshly ground black pepper and 5 ml (1 tsp) fennel seeds.

VARIATION

Add 2 red peppers, halved seeded and diced, and 5 ml (1 tsp) mild chilli seasoning to the onions.

TECHNIQUE

Sprinkle the polenta into the boiling salted water, whisking constantly to prevent lumps forming.

ASPARAGUS, BROAD BEAN AND PARMESAN FRITTATA

An Italian omelette which is cooked slowly over a low heat, the filling stirred into the eggs or scattered over the top; sometimes it is finished off under the grill. A frittata is served perfectly set, never folded. This recipe will serve 4 as a snack, or 2 persons as a meal.

SERVES 2-4

175 g (6 oz) small new
   potatoes
225 g (8 oz) asparagus
225 g (8 oz) frozen broad
   beans, thawed
6 eggs
salt and pepper
50 g (2 oz) freshly grated
   Parmesan cheese
45 ml (3 tbsp) chopped
   mixed fresh herbs, such as
   parsley, oregano and
   thyme
50 g (2 oz) butter

PREPARATION TIME
35 minutes
COOKING TIME
15-20 minutes
FREEZING
Not suitable

720-360 CALS PER SERVING

1. Cook the potatoes in boiling salted water for 15-20 minutes until tender. Allow to cool, then slice thickly.

2. Meanwhile, trim the asparagus, removing any woody parts of the stems. Steam for 12 minutes until tender, then plunge into cold water to set the colour and cool completely.

3. Slip the broad beans out of their waxy skins. Drain the asparagus, pat dry, then cut into short lengths. Mix with the broad beans.

4. Put the eggs in a bowl with a good pinch of salt, plenty of pepper and half of the Parmesan cheese. Beat thoroughly until evenly blended, then stir in the asparagus, broad beans and chopped herbs.

5. Melt 40 g (1½ oz) butter in a 25 cm (10 inch) non-stick heavy-based frying pan. When foaming, pour in the egg mixture. Turn down the heat to as low as possible. Cook for about 15 minutes, until the frittata is set and the top is still a little runny.

6. Preheat the grill. Scatter the cooked sliced potato over the frittata and sprinkle with the remaining Parmesan cheese. Dot with the rest of the butter.

7. Place under the hot grill to lightly brown the cheese and just set the top; don't allow it to brown too much or it will dry out. Slide the frittata onto a warmed dish and cut into wedges to serve.

VARIATION

Lay 4 slices of prosciutto over the top of the lightly set frittata and grill for 2-3 minutes until crisp.

TECHNIQUE

Once thawed, frozen broad beans can be removed easily from their skins. Pinch one end of the skin to squeeze out the bean.

BAKED FENNEL WITH LEMON AND OLIVES

Florence fennel bulbs are braised to tender sweetness with smoky black olives and lemon juice. Fennel has a slightly aniseed flavour which goes well with fish dishes and cuts the richness of stews and braised meat dishes. Celery can be cooked in the same way. This dish is equally delicious hot or cold.

SERVES 4

3 large fennel bulbs, or
   4 medium ones
90 ml (6 tbsp) olive oil
grated ring and juice of
   1 lemon
salt and pepper
12 black or green olives
30 ml (2 tbsp) chopped fresh
   parsley

PREPARATION TIME
15 minutes
COOKING TIME
45 minutes
FREEZING
Not suitable

225 CALS PER SERVING

1. Preheat the oven to 200°C (400°F) Mark 6. Trim the fennel and cut away any bruised parts. Cut off the fibrous tops, halve the bulbs lengthways and cut out the core. Cut larger bulbs into quarters.

2. Place the fennel halves or quarters cut-side up, in a baking dish. Mix the lemon rind and juice with the olive oil, salt and pepper.

3. Pour the lemon mixture over the fennel, scatter over the olives and bake in the oven for 15 minutes. Turn the fennel and bake for a further 15 minutes. Turn once more and bake for a final 15 minutes until tender. Serve sprinkled with the parsley.

NOTE: For a softer texture, blanch the fennel quarters in boiling water for 2 minutes and drain well before baking.

VARIATION

Use 2 fennel bulbs and 3 heads of chicory. Quarter the fennel and halve the chicory bulbs, removing the bitter core. Continue from stage 2, mixing the fennel and chicory together.

TECHNIQUE

Halve or quarter the fennel bulbs and cut out the core.

TOMATO AND AUBERGINE GRATIN

Tomato halves are baked with briefly fried thin aubergine slices and freshly grated Parmesan to make a pretty gratin which is full of flavour. This simple vegetable accompaniment goes well with most meat and poultry dishes. Alternatively, it can be served as a starter.

SERVES 4

1 medium aubergine
salt and pepper
450 g (1 lb) ripe red
   tomatoes
150 ml (¼ pint) olive oil
45 ml (3 tbsp) freshly grated
   Parmesan cheese

PREPARATION TIME
10 minutes, plus standing
COOKING TIME
25 minutes
FREEZING
Not suitable

420 CALS PER SERVING

1. Preheat the oven to 200°C (400°F) Mark 6. With a sharp knife, cut the aubergine into 3 mm (⅛ inch) slices. Place in a colander, sprinkling with salt, and leave for 30 minutes. Rinse well and pat dry with kitchen paper.

2. Halve the tomatoes horizontally. Heat half of the oil in a frying pan and briefly fry the aubergine slices in batches until golden brown on both sides. Add more oil to the pan as necessary. Drain on kitchen paper.

3. Arrange the tomato halves and aubergine slices in a shallow ovenproof dish. Season with salt and pepper and sprinkle with Parmesan.

4. Bake in the oven for 10-15 minutes until browned. Allow to cool slightly, then serve warm. Alternatively let cool completely and chill before serving, as a salad.

NOTE: The cooking time depends on the size of the tomatoes. If large, halve them, then place cut-side up in a roasting pan. Sprinkle with salt and olive oil and roast in the preheated oven for 15 minutes until beginning to soften. Arrange in the dish with the aubergines, pour on the pan juices, season and sprinkle with the Parmesan. Bake as above.

VARIATION

- Replace the aubergines with sliced courgettes.
- Add chopped fresh herbs, such as oregano, parsley or basil, if you like.

TECHNIQUE

Layer the aubergine slices in a colander, sprinkling them with salt. Leave to stand to degorge the bitter juices.

GARLIC POTATOES

Chunky 'chips' of potato are cooked with olive oil, garlic and herbs. Rosemary and thyme impart a wonderful woody aroma to the potatoes as they steam. It is essential to use waxy potatoes for this recipe as floury ones would disintegrate. Use a firm variety, such as Maris Piper, Desirée or Romano.

SERVES 4

575 g (1¼ lb) medium-sized waxy potatoes
90 ml (6 tbsp) olive oil
4 unpeeled garlic cloves
few fresh thyme or rosemary sprigs
25 g (1 oz) butter
crystal salt, for sprinkling

PREPARATION TIME
15 minutes
COOKING TIME
20 minutes
FREEZING
Not suitable

320 CALS PER SERVING

1. Cut the potatoes lengthwise into quarters, then place in a bowl of cold water. Rinse and pat dry with kitchen paper.

2. Heat the oil in a flameproof casserole or heavy-based pan and, when smoking hot, add the potatoes and garlic. Reduce the heat and fry the potatoes, turning, until browned on all sides. Stir in the herbs, cover tightly and allow the potatoes to cook in their own steam for 15 minutes.

3. Remove the lid and turn the heat up to evaporate any water and crisp the potatoes. Add the butter and toss gently.

4. Scatter with plenty of salt and garnish with thyme or rosemary sprigs to serve.

NOTE: It is important to rinse and dry the potatoes, to help prevent them from sticking during cooking.

VARIATION

Fry 125 g (4 oz) chopped derinded pancetta or unsmoked bacon with the potatoes at stage 2.

TECHNIQUE

Fry the potatoes and whole garlic cloves in the hot oil, turning constantly, until browned on all sides.

THREE CLASSIC SORBETS

This book would not be complete without three of the most refreshing sorbets imaginable! The Sicilian orange sorbet is delicately flavoured with exotic orange flower water and orange juice; strawberry sorbet has a hint of rich balsamic vinegar which is almost imperceptible but brings out the flavour of the strawberries; while melon sorbet is just a taste of sunshine!

EACH SORBET SERVES 4-6

MELON SORBET
about 900 g (2 lb) very ripe
    cantaloupe or other
    orange-fleshed melon
225 g (8 oz) caster sugar
juice of 1 lemon or 2 limes
1 egg white
ORANGE SORBET
200 g (7 oz) caster sugar
10 juicy oranges
30 ml (2 tbsp) orange flower
    water
1 egg white
STRAWBERRY SORBET
450 g (1 lb) fresh sweet
    strawberries
250 g (9 oz) caster sugar
15 ml (1 tbsp) balsamic
    vinegar
1 egg white

PREPARATION TIME
20 minutes per sorbet, plus
chilling
COOKING TIME
Nil
FREEZING TIME
3-4 hours

165-280 CALS PER SERVING

1. To make the melon sorbet, halve and deseed the melon, cutting out any bad parts. Scoop out the melon flesh into a blender or food processor. Process until smooth, then press through a sieve into a bowl. Cover and chill for 2-3 hours.

2. Pour 300 ml (½ pint) water into a saucepan, add the sugar and heat gently to dissolve. Boil for 1 minute. Cool, then chill.

3. Stir the syrup into the chilled melon, then add lemon or lime juice to taste. Beat the egg white until just frothy and whisk into the melon mixture. Freeze in an ice-cream maker for optimum results. Alternatively, pour into a shallow freezer tray and freeze until the sorbet is almost frozen. Mash well with a fork and refreeze until solid.

4. To make the orange sorbet, pour 200 ml (⅓ pint) water into a saucepan and add the sugar. Proceed as for step 2, but add the thinly pared rind of the oranges and their juice. Leave to cool, stir in the orange flower water, then chill. Strain, whisk in the egg white and freeze as in step 3.

5. To make the strawberry sorbet, pour 250 ml (9 fl oz) water into a saucepan and add the sugar. Proceed as in step 2. Meanwhile, wash and hull the strawberries. Place in a blender or food processor and process until smooth. Pass through a sieve, if liked. Chill.

6. Stir the syrup and balsamic vinegar into the strawberry purée, and beat in the egg white as in step 3. Freeze in the usual way.

NOTE: When making sorbets and ice creams it is best to have all the ingredients chilled before freezing – this speeds up the freezing process. Transfer the sorbets to the refrigerator 30 minutes before serving to soften slightly.

The melon must be as ripe as possible to ensure the intense sweet flavour.

TECHNIQUE

Pass the puréed melon through a sieve into a bowl.

RICE ICE CREAM

A superb creamy vanilla ice cream, with a barely perceptible granular texture. It seems to have originated in Sicily, famed for its ice cream, but is now popular all over Italy. In Sicily, rosewater, cinnamon and even ginger are used as flavourings. Fresh peaches and figs both go perfectly with the ice cream.

SERVES 8

125 g (4 oz) pudding rice (round-grain)

600 ml (1 pint) creamy milk (preferably Jersey)

175 g (6 oz) caster sugar

1 vanilla pod, split

600 ml (1 pint) double cream, chilled

15 ml (1 tbsp) orange flower water or rosewater

PREPARATION TIME
10 minutes
COOKING TIME
1 hour
FREEZING TIME
2 hours

530 CALS PER SERVING

1. Preheat the oven to 180°C (350°F) Mark 4. Put the rice in a flameproof casserole with the milk, sugar and vanilla pod. Bring to the boil, cover tightly and bake in the oven for about 1 hour until very tender.

2. Remove from the oven, discard the vanilla pod and cover the surface with greaseproof paper. Allow to cool, then chill in the refrigerator for at least 1 hour.

3. Stir the cream and orange flower water or rosewater into the chilled rice.

4. Freeze in an ice-cream maker according to the manufacturer's instructions until the consistency of whipped cream, then transfer to a freezerproof container and place in the freezer for at least 2 hours.

5. Transfer the ice cream to the refrigerator 1 hour before serving, to soften. Serve in scoops, with peaches or figs.

NOTE: If you do not have an ice cream machine, freeze the ice cream in a freezerproof container, whisking periodically during freezing to break down the ice crystals and ensure a smooth-textured result.

VARIATION

Instead of the vanilla pod, add 2.5 ml (½ tsp) ground cinnamon to the milk.

TECHNIQUE

Cover the surface of the cooked rice with a piece of greaseproof paper to prevent a skin forming as it cools.

PANNA COTTA WITH STRAWBERRY SAUCE

Panna cotta is a silky smooth, lightly set cream, originating from the Piedmont region of Italy, which produces such wonderful dairy products. Here it is served with a sweet/sour sauce of strawberries flavoured with a hint of balsamic vinegar. Serve the dessert with extra strawberries.

SERVES 4-5

300 ml (½ pint) mascarpone
300 ml (½ pint) double
  cream
finely pared rind of 1 orange
125 g (4 oz) caster sugar
1 vanilla pod, split
60 ml (4 tbsp) milk
10 ml (2 tsp) powdered
  gelatine
SAUCE
450 g (1 lb) strawberries
30 ml (2 tbsp) icing sugar
15 ml (1 tbsp) balsamic
  vinegar
TO SERVE
halved strawberries

PREPARATION TIME
45 minutes, plus setting
COOKING TIME
Nil
FREEZING
Not suitable

865-695 CALS PER SERVING

1. Put the mascarpone, cream, orange rind, sugar and vanilla pod in a saucepan. Place over a low heat until almost but not quite boiling, stirring occasionally. Remove from the heat and leave to infuse for 20 minutes.

2. Put the milk into another pan and sprinkle over the gelatine. Place over a very low heat until the gelatine is dissolved.

3. Stir the dissolved gelatine into the cream and mascarpone mixture. Bring to the boil, then immediately take off the heat and strain into a jug.

4. Lightly oil four or five 150 ml (¼ pint) ramekins or small moulds and pour in the cream mixture. Chill in the refrigerator for several hours or until set.

5. To make the strawberry sauce, hull and halve the strawberries. Place them in a saucepan with the icing sugar and 45 ml (3 tbsp) water. Heat slowly until the juices start to run. Transfer to a blender or food processor, add the balsamic vinegar and blend until smooth. Pass through a sieve to remove the seeds, if preferred. Pour into a bowl, cover and chill in the refrigerator for 3-4 hours until set.

6. To serve, carefully loosen the creams and turn out onto individual plates. Surround with the sauce and strawberries to decorate. Serve at once.

NOTE: If mascarpone is unobtainable, use double cream instead. The result will be less rich, but still delicious.

VARIATION

Caramelised Panna Cottas: Dissolve 90 ml (6 tbsp) granulated sugar in 30 ml (2 tbsp) water in a heavy-based pan over a low heat, then boil to a golden caramel. Quickly pour into the oiled moulds to coat evenly. Pour the hot cream on top and allow to set. Chill and turn out the next day.

TECHNIQUE

Divide the cream mixture evenly between lightly oiled moulds.

SEMI-FREDDO DI RICOTTA AL CAFFE

A semi-freddo is a dessert that is half frozen to give it a slightly thickened, creamy texture. Ricotta and mascarpone are sweetened, laced with rum and Tia Maria and flavoured with pulverised Italian coffee. The texture of the coffee gives an interesting texture, but you must buy espresso coffee which is *very finely* ground. Spooned into white demi-tasse cups, this is a delightful, rich dessert.

SERVES 6-8

350 g (12 oz) ricotta
   (at room temperature)
350 g (12 oz) mascarpone
   (at room temperature)
15 ml (1 tbsp) rum
45 ml (3 tbsp) Tia Maria or
   other coffee liqueur
5 ml (1 tsp) vanilla essence
30 ml (2 tbsp) espresso-
   ground Italian roast coffee
icing sugar, to taste
TO DECORATE
whipped cream
chocolate curls (see below)
bitter chocolate squares

PREPARATION TIME
20 minutes, plus freezing
COOKING TIME
Nil
FREEZING
Suitable: Up to 1 week

560-375 CALS PER SERVING

1. Beat the ricotta and mascarpone together in a bowl, using a wooden spoon. (Do not attempt to do this in a food processor or the mixture will go very runny.)

2. Beat in the rum, Tia Maria, vanilla essence and ground coffee. Add icing sugar to taste. Carefully spoon into demi-tasse cups or small ramekins, piling the mixture high.

3. Place in the freezer for 2 hours. Transfer to the refrigerator 30 minutes before serving to soften slightly. The dessert should be *only just* frozen or very chilled.

4. Just before serving, top each serving with a spoonful of whipped cream and a sprinkling of chocolate curls. Set on saucers and serve immediately, with squares of bitter chocolate.

NOTE: Ricotta is a light fresh cheese made from whey. If unavailable, use sieved cottage cheese instead.

CHOCOLATE CURLS: Spread melted plain chocolate on a marble slab to a depth of 5 mm (¼ inch). When just set, draw a fine-bladed knife across the chocolate at a 45° angle to shave off curls.

VARIATIONS

● Fold in 50 g (2 oz) toasted chopped hazelnuts before freezing.
● Fold 125 g (4 oz) grated dark bitter chocolate into the mixture before freezing.

TECHNIQUE

Beat the rum, liqueur, vanilla essence and finely ground coffee into the cheese mixture.

PANNETONE

This classic Italian favourite is really a cross between a bread and a cake. Light, yet buttery and rich, it is studded with dried fruit and candied peel. Because of the high butter content, pannetone keeps well. It is normally eaten with coffee, or a glass of dessert or fortified wine.

MAKES 10-12 SLICES

15 ml (1 tbsp) active dried
   yeast
150 ml (¼ pint) warm milk
450 g (1 lb) strong plain
   white flour
1 egg
4 egg yolks
10 ml (2 tsp) salt
75 g (3 oz) caster sugar
finely grated rind of 1 lemon
finely grated rind of
   1 orange
175 g (6 oz) unsalted butter,
   softened
75 g (3 oz) chopped mixed
   candied orange and citron
   peel
125 g (4 oz) raisins

PREPARATION TIME
25 minutes, plus rising
COOKING TIME
35 minutes
FREEZING
Suitable

415-320 CALS PER SERVING

1. Line a 15 cm (6 inch) deep cake tin with a double layer of non-stick baking parchment which projects 12 cm (5 inches) above the rim.

2. Dissolve the yeast in 60 ml (4 tbsp) warm milk. Cover and leave in a warm place for 10 minutes until frothy. Stir in 125 g (4 oz) flour and the remaining warm milk. Cover and leave to rise for 30 minutes.

3. Beat the egg and egg yolks together. Sift the remaining flour and salt onto the yeast mixture. Make a well in the centre and add the sugar, beaten eggs and citrus rinds. Mix to an elastic dough, adding a little more flour if necessary, but keeping the dough quite soft. Work in the softened butter.

4. Cover and leave to rise for 2-4 hours until doubled in volume. Meanwhile, chop the candied peel.

5. Preheat the oven to 200°C (400°F) Mark 6. Knock the dough down and knead in the chopped peel and raisins. Place in the prepared tin and cut an X on the top with a scalpel or very sharp knife. Cover and leave to rise until the dough is 2.5 cm (1 inch) above the top of the tin.

6. Bake in the oven for 15 minutes, then lower the heat to 180°C (350°F) Mark 4 and bake for a further 40 minutes until well risen and golden. Leave in the tin for 10 minutes, then transfer to a wire rack to cool.

7. Serve cut into horizontal slices. To store, replace the top and wrap the whole pannetone in cling film or foil. Keep in the refrigerator. Bring to room temperature to serve.

NOTE: Most sweet egg and butter enriched doughs take a long time to rise, so start them early in the day. Don't put them to rise in a very warm place once the butter has been been incorporated, or the butter will melt and the dough will be greasy.

TECHNIQUE

Leave the dough to rise in the tin until it is 2.5 cm (1 inch) above the rim.

BISCOTTI

These light, crunchy biscuits – studded with toasted almonds and with a hint of orange – are the perfect way to round off an Italian meal. They are traditionally served with a glass of *vin santo*, a sweet dessert wine from Tuscany. The only way to eat them is to dip them in the wine and munch! They are very more-ish!

MAKES ABOUT 50

175 g (6 oz) whole blanched almonds

15 ml (1 tbsp) coriander seeds

125 g (4 oz) unsalted butter, softened

200 g (7 oz) granulated sugar

2 eggs, beaten

finely grated rind of 1 orange

15 ml (1 tbsp) Grand Marnier or other orange liqueur

7.5 ml (1½ tsp) baking powder

2.5 ml (½ tsp) salt

about 350 g (12 oz) plain white flour

75 g (3 oz) coarse-grain polenta (ordinary or quick-cook)

PREPARATION TIME
25 minutes
COOKING TIME
45 minutes, plus cooling
FREEZING
Not suitable

90 CALS PER BISCUIT

1. Preheat the oven to 170°C (325°F) Mark 3. Spread the almonds on a baking sheet and toast in the oven for 5-10 minutes until golden. Allow to cool. Coarsely chop one third of the toasted nuts and mix with the whole ones. Lightly crush the coriander seeds.

2. In a bowl, cream the butter with the sugar until just mixed. Beat in the eggs, orange rind, liqueur, baking powder and salt. Stir in 275 g (10 oz) flour, the polenta, almonds and crushed coriander.

3. Turn the dough onto a floured work surface and knead until smooth, adding the remaining flour little by little, until the dough is soft but not sticky. It may not be necessary to add all of the flour.

4. Divide the dough into four equal pieces and roll each into a 5 cm (2 inch) wide, 2 cm (¾ inch) deep, sausage. Place these on 2 greased baking sheets and bake for about 35 minutes until just golden around the edges.

5. Carefully transfer to a wire rack. Allow to cool for 10 minutes, then cut diagonally into 1 cm (½ inch) thick slices. Place these slices, cut-side down, on the baking sheets and bake for another 10 minutes until golden brown. Transfer to a wire rack to cool completely. Store in an airtight tin for up to 1 week.

NOTE: Polenta is maize meal and can be bought in different grades. Use coarse meal for biscotti.

VARIATIONS

● Replace the almonds with pine nuts.

● Replace the almonds with hazelnuts and use 275 g (10 oz) plain flour sifted with 50 g (2 oz) cocoa powder.

● Replace the coriander with aniseed or fennel and use an anise liqueur, such as Pernod.

TECHNIQUE

Using a large sharp knife, cut the par-baked dough into 1 cm (½ inch) thick slices, using a single stroke to cut them cleanly.

PANFORTE DE SIENA

This rich, spicy, thin 'cake' is packed with candied peel, honey and nuts. Served in thin slices, after dinner or with coffee, panforte is a traditional Christmas treat throughout Italy. In Siena, its town of origin, every confectioner's shop has their own variation!

MAKES 12 SLICES

125 g (4 oz) whole blanched
   almonds
125 g (4 oz) whole skinned
   hazelnuts
125 g (4 oz) candied orange
   peel
125 g (4 oz) candied citron
   peel
50 g (2 oz) plain white flour
1.25 ml (¼ tsp) ground
   coriander
1.25 ml (¼ tsp) ground
   white pepper
1.25 ml (¼ tsp) ground
   nutmeg
1.25 ml (¼ tsp) ground
   cloves
5 ml (1 tsp) ground
   cinnamon
125 g (4 oz) granulated
   sugar
225 g (8 oz) thin honey
25 g (1 oz) butter
icing sugar, for dusting

PREPARATION TIME
45 minutes
COOKING TIME
35 minutes
FREEZING
Not suitable

265 CALS PER SLICE

1. Preheat the oven to 180°C (350°F) Mark 4. Grease and line a 20 cm (8 inch) springform cake tin with non-stick baking parchment (see note). Spread the almonds and hazelnuts on a baking tray and bake in the oven for 10-15 minutes until golden brown.

2. Let the nuts cool slightly, then chop roughly and place in a medium bowl. Lower the oven temperature to 150°C (300°F) Mark 2.

3. Finely chop the orange and citron peel and add to the nuts. Sift the flour and spices together into the bowl. Stir to mix.

4. Put the sugar, honey and butter in a saucepan and heat gently, stirring occasionally, until dissolved. Bring to the boil and boil steadily until the syrup reaches the soft ball stage and registers 117°C (242°F) on a sugar thermometer. Quickly stir in the nut mixture, pour into the prepared tin and smooth the surface with an oiled potato masher (see technique); work quickly otherwise the mixture will set.

5. Bake in the oven for 35 minutes; the cake won't be brown or set at this stage. Transfer the tin to a wire rack; the cake will harden as it cools.

6. When cold, carefully remove the tin and baking parchment.

7. Dredge the panforte with icing sugar. Store in an airtight tin for up to 1 month. Serve cut into thin slices.

NOTE: You can line the cake tin with edible rice paper if you prefer; this makes it easier to turn the cake out. Don't use greaseproof paper – it simply won't work!

CITRON PEEL: This is the candied peel of the citron – a citrus fruit that resembles a large knobbly lemon. It has a very thick rind, but little flesh.

VARIATION

Replace the almonds with walnuts and add 50 g (2 oz) chopped dried figs (not ready-to-eat) and 30 ml (2 tbsp) cocoa powder.

TECHNIQUE

Use an oiled potato masher to level and smooth the surface, working quickly as the mixture soon sets hard.

If you would like further information about the **Good Housekeeping Cookery Club**, please write to: Penny Smith, Ebury Press, Random House, 20 Vauxhall Bridge Road, London SW1V 2SA.